VOLUME 1

PSALMS

SONGS FROM THE HEART

D1580949

10 Publishing
a division of 10 of those.com

First published in Great Britain in 2018

British Library Cataloguing in Publication Data

A record for this book is available from the British Library

ISBN: 978-1-912373-40-6
Designed by Diane Warnes
Printed in the UK

10Publishing, a division of 10ofthose.com
Unit C, Tomlinson Road, Leyland, PR25 2DY, England
Email: info@10ofthose.com
Website: www.10ofthose.com

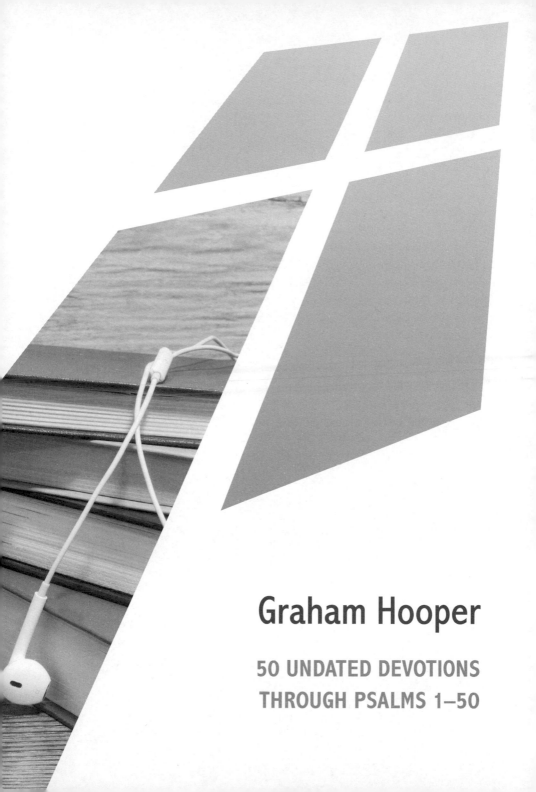

Graham Hooper

50 UNDATED DEVOTIONS
THROUGH PSALMS 1–50

# INTRODUCTION

Structure

The book of psalms is a collection of 150 psalms (songs and poems), divided up into five smaller 'books' as follows:

- Book 1: Psalms 1–41;
- Book 2: Psalms 42–72;
- Book 3: Psalms 73–89;
- Book 4: Psalms 90–106; and
- Book 5: Psalms 107–150.

There are some identifiable groupings of psalms around specific themes, and it is helpful to understand the overall context when we study one particular psalm within any one of these groupings. For example:

- the focus of Psalms 93–100 is on the Lord as the great King;
- Psalms 113–118 form the Hallel, traditionally sung on Passover night;
- Psalms 120–134 are the 'songs of ascents' for pilgrims; and
- Psalms 146–150 close out the book with songs of praise.

Recurring themes

Some powerful themes recur though the psalms: the sovereignty, justice and faithful love of God; why evil people seem to prosper; personal trust and commitment to the promises of God in the face of difficulty; and the greatness of the power of the Creator God – the rock, the refuge, the fortress and the one worthy of our trust, our praise and our worship.

There is also some repetition of words and phrases and even of some whole psalms. For example:

- Psalm 53 is the same as Psalm 14 apart from a few details and the greater part of verse 5 of Psalm 53;
- Psalm 70 is practically identical to Psalm 40:13–17; and
- Psalm 108 is made up of two psalm endings: 57:7–11 and 60:5–12.

Style

The psalms are poetry and songs. Many contain poetic imagery. They include praise, thanksgiving, questioning, requests and laments, but rarely instruction.

Some psalms are written in the form of acrostics. For example, in the very long Psalm 119 each section begins with a different letter of the Hebrew alphabet. In Psalm 34 each verse begins with a different letter.

Who wrote the psalms?

Many of the psalms tell us (in their header) who wrote them. 73 of the 150 psalms are attributed to David, the shepherd boy who became king. Several were written by Asaph, a temple musician, and some by the Sons of Korah, a guild of temple officials. Others are attributed to authors such as Solomon (Ps. 72) and Moses (Ps. 90), or are unattributed (for example, Ps. 1).

When were the psalms written?

The simple answer seems to be over a period between the time of David (1000 BC approximately) – though with the psalm attributed to Moses possibly earlier – and the years after the exile of the people of Judah into Babylon (300–500 BC). In some cases the headers tell us about the circumstances in which the psalms were written. For example, the note at the head of Psalm 51 tells us that David's famous prayer of repentance was a response to God after the prophet Nathan had confronted him with his sins of adultery and murder. Similarly, we are told that David wrote Psalm 3 while on the run from his own son Absalom who was trying to kill him.

The psalms in the New Testament

The psalms formed the 'hymnbook' of Israelite religion before the time of Christ. There are over 50 quotations from the psalms in the New Testament – more than any other Old Testament book. The frequent use of quotations from 'messianic psalms' in the book of Acts shows us how many of the psalms prophetically point to the coming Messiah and have a specific fulfilment in Jesus Christ. Jesus frequently quoted from the psalms as part of God's Word and as revealing truth about himself (see, for example, Luke 24:44).

The psalms in the Christian church

From the very beginning of the Christian church the psalms have been accepted as part of the divine revelation, and have been used widely in personal and corporate prayers and praise for the past two thousand years. As we read the psalms, therefore, with the New Testament in our hand, we can expect to learn more about Jesus.

The value and use of the psalms today

The psalms form part of our inspired Scripture. When we read them with an open, prayerful heart, we will find that the God who inspired them will continue to speak through them today. He speaks to us where we are at. He challenges us, encourage us, and stirs up our faith and commitment to him.

Like all good poetry, the psalms engage the heart and emotions as well as the mind. Their continuing widespread use in study, private prayer and communal worship is testament to their ongoing appeal to believers in every culture. Whatever our experience at any given time in the emotional spectrum, from elated joy to deep depression, we can find a psalm which echoes our experience. It's no wonder that at times when we find it hard to read or study other parts of the Bible – when we are tired, sick or depressed – it is to the psalms that we turn. They help us to pray, to worship and to reflect on God and our relationship with him.

As we read them, study them, pray them or sing them, our God delights to use them to reveal to us more about himself and to deepen our knowledge of him.

Studying the psalms with this guide

Read the psalm for the day and then the notes and questions contained in the study guide. Ask yourself some questions as you read:

- What do I learn about God in this verse and passage?
- What did this mean to the original hearers?
- What does it mean for me in the twenty-first century?
- How can I respond with practical action?

Two ways to live

Where is true happiness to be found? In a healthy life, with enough money to pursue our dreams? In success in our chosen field? This opener to the book of psalms presents a surprisingly different answer. It is found in delighting in 'the law [Torah, that is the "teaching"] of the LORD' (v. 2); in a desire to learn from God through reading and meditating on his Word, the Bible.

As we understand and seek to obey God's Word, we find it changes our life. We start to want to live differently in the best possible sense. We see in verse 1 that the blessed (that is, happy) person, later called the righteous (vv. 5–6), does not:

- 'walk in step with the wicked' – habitially following the majority in doing what is contrary to the Word of God;

- 'stand in the way that sinners take' – identifying with those whose beliefs and behaviours are obviously contrary to God's law; or,

- 'sit in the company of mockers' – ridiculing and dismissing faith, and 'rubbishing' those seeking to live a godly life.

This happy person is pictured as a growing tree (v. 3), continually drawing life from the stream. Its leaves do not wither. It is fruitful, healthy and useful – a beautiful and atractive picture of practical godliness.

One alternative

By contrast, 'the wicked', those who want no part in God and have no interest in his Word, are like the chaff that the wind blows away' (v. 4). Their lives have no lasting value or substance.

Two outcomes (vv. 5–6)

Like many of Jesus' parables, this psalm calls us to choose. There is no compromise, no 'third way'. There is the way of 'the righteous', or there is the way of the 'wicked'. The outcomes of each path are presented starkly (v. 6).

REFLECTION

Two ways of living; two very different outcomes. This psalm is neither a prayer nor a praise song, but it presents us with a choice. The first word of this psalm is 'blessed' and the last word is 'perish': that seems to summarise the two contrasting ways to live. Each of us has to choose.

The Messiah and rebellion against God

On the surface, it often appears that most non-Christians are indifferent, or simply ignorant, of the Christian faith. In popular western culture religion is seen as a matter of personal choice, never to be inflicted on others. But when we look a little deeper, we find a darker picture of antagonism behind the veneer. Humankind is opposed to God and rejects his authority. Individually, our sinfulness and estrangement from God lead us to fight against him.

Moving on from Psalm 1, we are confronted with this darker scene. The idyllic picture of faith and godliness in Psalm 1 changes to an ugly view of the world in rebellion against God.

Why is this so? 'Why do the nations conspire and the peoples plot in vain?' (v. 1). Why do those opposed to God 'band together' to try to 'throw off their shackles' (vv. 2–3)? Why, when the Son of God came to this earth, did his own people reject him (Luke 19:14)? Why are God's people persecuted somewhere on the planet in every age?

More importantly, how does the Lord respond to this (vv. 4–6)? In two ways. First, he speaks. Actually, he laughs! (v. 4). As a parent might laugh at a petulant child throwing a tantrum, so God laughs at humankind's pathetic attempt to dispense with God in *his* own world. Fighting against God in any generation and in any society is ultimately 'in vain' (v. 1). Then he rebukes them in his anger (v. 5), a terrifying prospect for those who fight against him.

Finally, God acts (vv. 6–10): 'I have installed my king on Zion' (v. 6). David and his successors were mostly flawed leaders. This psalm points emphatically to Jesus, the coming Messiah, God's own Son. He will deliver his people and provide a refuge for them. It is no coincidence that this psalm, and Psalm 110, are the most quoted psalms in all the New Testament (see for example Acts 4:23–26).

REFLECTION

This very confronting psalm ends with great reassurance for all who take up God's gracious offer of reconciliation with his Son: 'Blessed are all who take refuge in him' (v. 12).

The God who 'lifts my head high'

When we are dispirited, our heads go down. Picture a defeated army, a file of refugees leaving their home or even a losing football team. Their body language tells us how they feel. But God lifts up our heads as he answers prayer, delivers us, encourages us, and strengthens us to go forward.

David, who wrote this psalm, was on the run from his own son Absalom, who had usurped David's throne and was out to kill him (2 Sam. 15:13–31). So David pours out his heart to God. He is surrounded by enemies (v. 1) and mocked by people who regarded him as out of favour with God: 'Many are saying of me, "God will not deliver him"'(v. 2). They were laughing at David's expectation that God would come to help him. He was certainly not experiencing the blessed life promised in Psalm 1 or the victory promised in Psalm 2. It is in this state that he turns to the Lord as his 'shield' (protector) and 'the One who lifts my head high' (v. 3).

As David kept calling out to the Lord (v. 4), his prayer was answered. We are not told how, but one of the practical outcomes was that he was now able to sleep and wake up with new energy: 'I lie down and sleep; I wake again, because the LORD sustains me' (v. 5). David, still facing his enemies (v. 7), is now confident – not in himself, but in the Lord. Wonderfully, he is no longer gripped by fear (v. 6). In this confidence he prays for God to act (v. 7). He is now sure that it is only the Lord who will deliver him (v. 7).

His final prayer is not for himself, but for all God's people. He asks that they will experience for themselves, as he has, answered prayer, renewed faith and the blessing of God (v. 8).

REFLECTION

When our heads are down, when we are fearful, disillusioned, feeling threatened and unable to sleep, let's pray this psalm for ourselves and remember that Jesus, great King David's greater Son, brings all of God's blessings to us.

DAY 4

Facing the night

Danger, pain and problems are usually much harder to cope with at night. When it's dark, when we are physically tired, when we are gripped by worries and fears, then sleep is hard to come by. Turning our eyes towards God at the end of the day helps us get life back into proportion before we try to sleep.

This psalm begins with David in real distress as night approaches, but it ends on a joyful note. It flows from prayer, to questions, to statements and back to prayer. He begins by asking God to hear his prayer, relieve his distress and show him mercy (v. 1).

David is distressed because his leadership and authority have been challenged, and his enemies have made false promises to the people (v. 2). So he asks, 'How long?' (v. 2). Yet this question isn't directed to God (as for example in Psalm 13), but rather to his enemies. How long would they go on attacking him and his reputation? How long will they continue worshipping false gods? He reminds them that he is God's person (v. 3). God has called him to his position of authority and answers his prayers. He urges those who doubt this to get their own lives sorted out with God (v. 4) and to put their trust in the Lord (v. 5).

Finally, David turns again to the Lord, asking him to shine his face on his people (v. 6) who were longing for better times. They wanted to know the smile of God on their life and the blessing of God in a tangible way (v. 6). But David knows that true prosperity and blessing can only come from the Lord. So he asks God for the joy which only God can give, a joy greater than can be gained from any material prosperity (v. 7).

REFLECTION

David commits himself to the Lord as he goes to sleep: 'In peace I will lie down and sleep, for you alone LORD, make me dwell in safety' (v. 8). If we are fearful and under pressure, this is a good psalm to make our own before we sleep.

DAY 5

A morning prayer

Some people are able to leap out of bed in the morning ready to face the day. Others of us awake more slowly. Either way, it's good to begin each day with prayer, committing the day to God, seeking his strength and asking him to guide us.

While Psalms 3 and 4 seem to have been written in the evening (see 3:5 and 4:8), Psalm 5 is a morning prayer: 'In the morning, LORD, you hear my voice; in the morning I lay my requests before you and wait expectantly' (v. 3). But some mornings bring more troubles than joys. David begins his day with a cry for help (vv. 1–3), because he is surrounded by enemies and desperate for relief. Then:

He remembers God's holy character

... he knows God is not pleased with wickedness and will not accept the arrogant, liars, deceitful or bloodthirsty into his presence (vv. 4–6).

He rejoices

... in the great privilege he has as a believer to come into the presence of God (v. 7) and he asks for God's continued guidance to keep him on the right path (v. 8).

He prays for justice

... which will always have two sides: punishment of the guilty and acquittal of the innocent. So he prays first that evil doers, whose words cannot be trusted (v. 9), will be declared guilty and banished from God's presence (v. 10). He prays second that 'all' (notice he is now pleading for justice for others, not just for himself) 'who take refuge in you be glad; let them ever sing for joy' (v. 11). When justice is done, when the innocent and repentant find refuge in God, there is reason for joy, not just a grim satisfaction that right has prevailed.

REFLECTION

David (like Jesus in 1 Peter 2:23) trusts himself to God 'who judges justly'. So should we. David also prays for others, that they too will experience God's protection and justice. So should we. As we begin our day, let's also remind ourselves, 'Surely, LORD, you bless the righteous; you surround them with your favour as with a shield' (v. 12).

Fear and sorrow

Whom do you turn to when you are fearful or in deep sorrow? If you have a true friend, a marriage partner or a family member who you can confide in, then you are truly blessed. But what if you are alone? What then?

David was alone and he was terrified (vv. 1–3), not just because of his circumstances, but because he couldn't escape the thought that they were a sign of God's displeasure: 'LORD do not rebuke me in your anger' (v. 1). He was exhausted with grief, in physical pain and in deep distress (vv. 2–3). He pleads with God, 'How long ...?' (v. 3); how long is this going to last?

David was alone in human terms, but he knew he still had a divine companion who was not going to leave him. So he calls on God's loving commitment to him (v. 4). David doesn't want to die in a state of fear (v. 5). He tells God in his prayer exactly how he is feeling: 'I am worn out from my groaning. All night long I flood my bed with weeping and drench my couch with tears' (v. 6). Lack of sleep, on top of all his other problems, was taking its physical toll. David, the great warrior, was near to a complete breakdown: 'My eyes grow weak with sorrow; they fail because of all my foes' (v. 7).

But, after bringing his life and troubles before the Lord in prayer, there is a radical change in David's outlook. It's not a superficial 'glossing over' of deep problems, but a growing confidence that the Lord is there. He has heard and answered David's prayers for mercy and help (v. 9) and he will deal with David's enemies (v. 10). So David turns to face his enemies, and his fears, with renewed strength and courage (v. 8).

REFLECTION

Notice the telling phrase 'the LORD has heard my weeping' (v. 8). This is a wonderfully tender and encouraging insight. We don't need carefully articulated prayers to attract God's attention. He hears the groaning of our heart (Rom. 8:26–27). He even 'hears' our weeping.

Justice

David in trouble again; David turning to God again. Is that starting to sound familiar? As we read through the psalms, we find it's a recurring pattern, and it's one which resonates with many of us as our troubles remind us of our dependence on God and our daily need of him.

Injustice abounds

David is fearful that those pursuing him will kill him (v. 2), so he cries out to God for help (v. 1). He is carrying a burning feeling of injustice. What has he done to deserve this? He challenges God to treat him fairly (vv. 3–5). Specifically, he asks God to:

- rise up in anger against his enemies (v. 6);

- vindicate him because, in this situation at least, he feels he has done no wrong (v. 8); and

- end the violence and 'make the righteous secure' (v. 9).

David acknowledges that God is righteous (v. 9), but that conviction is being sorely tested in the pressure cooker of his experience.

God is a righteous judge

This psalm emphasises God's righteousness and justice (vv. 6, 8, 9, 11, 17). He will deliver the righteous and defeat evil (v. 11). If we do evil, then evil will result. If we 'sow' evil, we will reap disillusionment, trouble and violence (vv. 14–16). The all-powerful 'God Most High' (v. 10) is a righteous judge, who will certainly act against his enemies (vv. 12–13). Like David, our faith may be tested as we see injustice in the world and experience injustice ourselves. When we are tempted to think that God is treating us or others unfairly, then this psalm reminds us that God will work out his justice in his time. He is a shield, a refuge and a Saviour (vv. 1, 10) to those who trust him.

REFLECTION

David begins and ends this psalm in confidence, faith and thankfulness for all that God is to him in his time of need (vv. 1, 17). He begins with prayer and ends with praise because he has turned his thoughts on the Lord, cleared his thinking and found renewed strength and hope.

The big picture

Sometimes we need to lift our eyes to see the 'big picture'. We may get so wrapped up in our selves, and in our daily routine, that we no longer see clearly the greatness of God. It's like looking through a telescope the wrong way round: God seems small and far away, and our problems loom large. We get things out of proportion.

So after several laments (Ps. 3–7) about the state of the world and the pressures on his own life, David focuses on the big picture – the glory of God and the grace of God to human beings.

The glory of God (vv. 1–3)

The psalm begins and ends gazing on the almighty power of the Lord (vv. 1, 9). David must have been looking up at the night sky (v. 3). As he reflects on the vastness of the universe, the awesome greatness of God and the seeming insignificance of human life in comparison, he asks, 'what is mankind that you are mindful of them, human beings that you care for them?' (v. 4)?

The grace of God (vv. 4–8)

And yet God does care. He uses even the testimony of the weak to defeat the strong (v. 2; Matt. 21:16). He has called us to a privileged position (vv. 5–8): made only 'a little lower than the angels' (v. 5) and ruler over the creation (see Gen. 1:26–28). But the full realisation of this is yet in the future. We have messed up this world and we are certainly not in full control of the forces in the creation. We are sinful and subject to disease, danger and death. But the New Testament shows how Jesus is the perfect fulfilment of this calling (Heb. 2:6–9), the protype of God's new creation. What is idealised about human beings in Psalm 8 is true of Jesus. Through him, we too will be 'crowned … with glory and honour' (v. 5) when he returns in his glory.

REFLECTION

What do we learn from this psalm about God; about human beings; and about Jesus? See Hebrews 2:5–9.

Two realities

Every day, the Christian believer lives with two realities. First, the power, love and justice of God; and second, the ever present reality of sin and evil. Jesus made clear that this was the way it would be until he comes. So we pray, as Jesus taught us, 'Yours is the kingdom, the power and the glory'. We also pray, 'Deliver us from evil'.

David knew these two realities. As he worships God, and thanks God for help and deliverance (vv. 1–6), he is also very conscious of the ongoing pressure of evil in this world (v. 13).

He begins by rejoicing in a past victory and the defeat of his enemies (vv. 1–6). The focus then changes to the Lord's rule over all the earth. He is a just judge and a refuge for all those in trouble (vv. 7–12). Verse 10 is a highlight: 'Those who know your name trust in you, for you, LORD, have never forsaken those who seek you.' For that reason we are encouraged to sing praises to God and to 'proclaim among the nations what he has done' (v. 11).

David next calls God's attention again to his many enemies. He cries out for God to rescue him from 'the gates of death' (v. 14). Those who reject the authority of God and 'forget him' will reap what they sow (vv. 15, 17), because the Lord is manifestly just (v. 16). He is also always caring for those in trouble. (v. 18).

David is not just wrapped up in himself. He has a heart for others and for the glory of God to be seen in the world. So he asks God to reveal his power and justice on a larger scale, to show the nations the folly of living without regard to the Lord (v. 20).

REFLECTION

God is in charge. Evil is still present. Every generation lives with these two realities (see Matt. 13:24–43). So this psalm speaks to us today as it has done in every generation since David wrote it. See also Jesus' words in John 16:33.

The question 'why?'

When troubles come, when we see cruelty and injustice in the world, we naturally ask, 'Why?' 'Why did God allow this to happen?' Or, more personally, 'Why did he allow it to happen to me?'

The psalms are full of questions. Some ask, 'How long' before God will answer their prayers (see Ps. 4 and 13). This psalm asks, 'Why?' In this case David is not seemingly concerned with injustices meted out to *him*, but rather with the unjust suffering of the helpless and disadvantaged. If David cares so much, then surely God must care also. David questions God's seeming inactivity and even disinterest in all the bad stuff happening in the world: 'Why, LORD, do you stand far off? Why do you hide yourself in times of trouble?' (v. 1).

David sees evil people boasting (v. 3), exploiting the weak (v. 2) and having no interest in God at all (v. 4). They lie (v. 7) and ruthlessly exploit and attack innocent and helpless people (vv. 8–10). They are full of self-confidence (v. 6) and are convinced that God does not see or is not concerned about how they live (vv. 6, 11).

David pleads with God to intervene (vv. 12–18): 'Arise, LORD! Lift up your hand ... ' (v. 12). 'Why does the wicked man revile God? Why does he say to himself, "He won't call me to account?"' (v. 13).

He ends by asking God to remember the helpless: surely God sees their trouble; surely he is 'the helper of the fatherless' (v. 14). He pleads with God to put a stop to the evil and to call those responsible to account (v. 15). He reminds himself, and us, that God is in charge, that he does care and that he does answer prayer.

REFLECTION

'It isn't fair. Why did God allow that injustice to happen? Why did those good people suffer so much? Why do evil people seem to get away with it?' How does this psalm help us think about these timeless questions? See also 1 Peter 4:12–19.

Under attack

The world can be a dangerous place. Right now you may be in a situation where you are afraid of physical attack. David wrote this psalm while in just such a situation. Even if you are living in reasonable safety, the Bible warns that every Christian is involved in spiritual warfare which we need to fight with spiritual weapons (Eph. 6:1–11) – rather than with bombs and guns. Whether the attack is physical or spiritual, this psalm speaks to us with the encouragement to look to the Lord and take refuge in him (vv. 1, 7).

Safety (vv. 1–3)

David is under attack. Evil powers are at work in the world targeting 'the upright in heart' (v. 2). This attack is intentional and destructive. It aims to undermine the very foundations of peaceful society: 'When the foundations are being destroyed, what can the righteous do?' (v. 3). David faces the strength and evil intent of the forces arrayed against him. The certainties of life seem to have gone. He takes refuge in the Lord, knowing that all human places of safety are useless in the face of such an onslaught (see also Prov. 18:10).

Eyes on the Lord (vv. 4–7)

David turns his eyes resolutely to the Lord, who is in his holy temple and on his heavenly throne (v. 4). This helps him see the evil attacks in the right perspective. He recognises that the Lord sees everything and everyone (v. 4). God hates the wicked but 'examines [tests] the righteous' (v. 5; see also Ps. 139:23–24). David concludes, 'For the LORD is righteous, he loves justice; the upright will see his face' (v. 7).

REFLECTION

When we are under attack, we are wise to look to the Lord and find strength in him, rather than try to battle on with only our own resources. The Lord is a place of safety for the believer. Indeed, ultimately he is the only place of safety. When we come to him, we want more than just a safe place in our trouble. We want to 'see his face' (v. 7).

Truth and lies

A bleak prospect

Secular materialism, which tries to dispense with God and ridicule Christian faith, is a truly bleak prospect for the human race. In a 'post–truth' society, truth is no longer believed or even valued. We might cynically observe that in a world of lies, propaganda and political spin, the shameless, convincing liar can win the day. In a very different culture, some 3,000 years ago, David was experiencing lies and propaganda aimed at destroying him and his reputation.

So he prays: 'Help, LORD, for no one is faithful any more ...' (v. 1). 'Everyone lies to their neighbour'; they flatter and deceive (v. 2). As we look out on the world and listen to the daily news, it may seem like that to us, at least on a bad day. Here, David sees betrayal and deception on every side (vv. 1–2). He sees people lying and boasting and shaking their fists at God: 'who is lord over us?' they say (v. 4).

The Word of the Lord

Standing against this barrage of lies and evil is the powerful unchanging Word of the Lord, eternally true, flawless, 'like silver purified in a crucible, like gold refined several times'

(v. 6). God's Word is 'the real thing', honest, powerful and valuable above all things.

So David prays, 'May the LORD silence all flattering lips and every boastful tongue' (v. 3) and he prophesies that the Lord will now act to protect the poor 'from those who malign them' (v. 5). Notice that when God speaks here, it is to show his concern for the weak and those exploited and abused by the words and actions of boastful, proud people who reject God's authority – those 'who freely strut about when what is vile is honoured by the human race' (v. 8).

The psalm ends with confident trust in the Lord that in every generation: 'You, LORD, will keep the needy safe and will protect us for ever from the wicked' (v. 7).

REFLECTION

How is the Word of God described elsewhere in Scripture? (See for example Ps. 119:105; John 17:17; Eph. 6:17; Heb. 4:12).

How long?

In the psalms we learn that it's OK to pour out our soul to God and ask him the hard questions. We don't need to pretend that we know all the answers, however wise we may think we are or however well we think we know our Bible. Some psalms begin with the question, 'Why?' (see for example Ps. 10). This one asks, 'How long, LORD?' (see also 74:10; 89:46).

This questioning, repeated four times (vv. 1–2), is obviously much more than just intellectual curiosity. It springs from deep loneliness and pain, an experience with which we may readily identify when we ask God, 'How long do I have to wait for an answer to my prayer? How long do I have to put up with this situation?'

In his pain and perplexity, David longs for a greater awareness of God: 'Look on me and answer ... Give light to my eyes' (v. 3). He prays that God would act so that his enemies did not have the satisfaction of gloating over his failure (v. 4). He feels close to death, overcome by the opposition arrayed against him, and pleads with God to look upon him and answer him. Otherwise he fears that he will die with his enemies rejoicing at his failure.

'*But ...* ' is a powerful word and we find it many times in the psalms to highlight a turnround in thinking and attitide as David is enabled to focus on God rather than on his problems. David had already 'turned the corner' in praying to God about his troubles (v. 3). Here is the second turning point: 'But I trust in your unfailing love' (v. 5). This is the solid rock on which David bases his confidence: the unfailing, steadfast love of God.

REFLECTION

We can surely learn from David here. In the depths of despair he turns to God and tells God his great need. He doesn't get a clear answer to his 'how long?' question, but he does remind himself of God's unfailing love and so ends on a note of confidence and joy. How much more should we! See also 1 Peter 1:3–9.

The fool

It's common for atheists to denigrate Christian faith and accuse those who believe in an invisible God as being misguided fools. But if God created the world, which the Bible reveals that he did, and if he will hold us all to account, as the Bible affirms he will, then it's hard to imagine greater foolishness than a human being, with a short life span on this earth, insisting that God does not exist! So this psalm begins: 'The fool says in his heart, "There is no God"' (v. 1).

The state of the world

Like Psalm 12, this psalm paints a dark picture. Turning away from God inevitably leads to rejection of God's laws and a slide into evil and chaos (Rom. 1:28–32). Godless people foolishly persecute God's people (v. 4) and frustrate the plans of the poor (v. 6), but they have their own more serious problems. Deep down, there is a deep dread, an angst, an emptiness in the soul (v. 5) that comes from being out of touch with God and fighting against him.

Where is God to be found in all this mess?

First, the psalm pictures the Lord looking 'down from heaven on all mankind' (v. 2), searching for anyone who understands, anyone who seeks God or who does good (vv. 2–3) and concluding that there is 'not even one' (v. 3).[2] Second, the psalmist sees that God is still 'present in the company of the righteous' (v. 5). There is a paradox here. If no one is good, then who are the righteous? The psalm points us to the answer: they are those who rely on God's saving grace and go to him as their refuge (vv. 6–7)

REFLECTION

The New Testament develops two major themes from this psalm: the foolishness of supposed 'human wisdom' (1 Cor. 1:18–25) and the universal problem of human sinfulness (Rom. 3:23). Both point us to the cross of Jesus, which seems foolishness to unbelievers, but which is the power and wisdom of God and God's way of salvation for sinners (1 Cor. 1:21–24).

DAY 15

Inward purity ... outward godliness

By contrast with Psalm 14, which pictures the fool who 'says in his heart, "There is no God"' (14:1), Psalm 15 describes a truly godly person. It's an attractive picture of someone without a trace of religious hypocrisy. It is similar in that sense to Psalm 1, but has a question-and-answer format.

Question (v. 1)

'LORD, who may dwell in your sacred tent? Who may live on your holy mountain?' (v. 1). In other words, 'Who may enter and live in the presence of God without fear?' (see also Ps. 24).

Answer (vv. 2–5)

It is the one:

- 'whose way of life is blameless, who does what is righteous' (v. 2). In other words, those whose actions are consistent with the character of God; and

- 'who speaks the truth from the heart' (v. 2). This means no slander, no putting down others behind their back, no nasty innuendo which discredits others (v. 3).

Such an individual will also honour those who fear the Lord (v. 4), keeping a promise 'even when it hurts' (v. 4), and not exploiting the poor when lending money or taking bribes to pervert the course of justice (v. 5).

It's a beautiful picture of someone who is perfectly whole, whose 'inner life' is in tune with God and whose outward behaviour expresses that reality (see Matt. 15:11, 18–19).

REFLECTION

Who can live up to this standard? The Bible's answer would be 'no one' (see Ps. 12:1–2 and 14:2–3). Only Jesus lived the perfect life pictured here. So this list isn't given to us as a series of boxes to be ticked to get our entrance ticket to heaven. It's not prescribing salvation by works or our own moral goodness. That would be to contradict the rest of the psalms and indeed the rest of the Bible. It is only by the grace of God that any of us can enter the presence of God and be accepted (Col. 1:12–13). But once we are accepted, this psalm (like the Sermon on the Mount in Matt. 5–8) shows us the way God calls us to live, with our outward behaviour consistent with the new inward reality of a changed heart.

Living in hope

What do we mean by hope? Wishful thinking, as in 'I hope the weather improves soon'? Or forward planning, as in 'I hope to get a new job next year'? In both cases the outcome is uncertain, however much we 'hope for the best'! The Bible meaning of 'hope' is very different. It means reliance on the promises of God. The outcome is certain. We simply look forward to God fulfilling his promises with expectancy, longing and patience. This psalm is full of this sort of hope. It's a wonderful 'breathing space' from the ongoing troubles of Psalms 3–7, 8–14 and of 17–18 which follow.

Hope in life after death

David has a glimspe of life after death. This will be a continuation of his relationship with the Lord begun on earth: 'you will not abandon me to the realm of the dead, nor will you let your faithful one see decay' (v. 10). He looks forward to being with the Lord forever (v. 11).

Hope in the coming Messiah

The use of Psalm 16 in the New Testament tells us this is a messianic psalm, pointing towards the coming of the Christ, the true anointed king.

Both Peter (Acts 2:25–28) and Paul (Acts 13:35) quote from this psalm in testifying about the resurrection of Jesus.

Hope in the present

'You make known to me the path of life' (v. 11). God shows us the path *to* life: eternal life, living with him forever. He also sets a path *of* life for us to follow here on earth.

REFLECTION

Why is David so hopeful? It's because his whole life is centred on the Lord. The Lord is his refuge (v. 1), his portion and cup (v. 5). The Lord makes him secure (v. 5), provides good things for him (v. 6) and guides him (v. 7). David keeps looking to the Lord in faith: 'I keep my eyes always on the LORD. With him at my right hand I will not be shaken' (v. 8). He also looks forward with hope: 'you will fill me with joy in your pesence' (v. 11).

Injustice and opposition

'It's not fair'; someone else gets the credit for your efforts, or you get the blame for someone else's mistakes. These are common experiences in most workplaces and in many families! Worse than that is to be 'trolled', bullied or otherwise persecuted without cause. Injustice *and* opposition is a painful and damaging combination. That's what David was facing in this psalm.

Unjustly dealt with? (vv. 1–5)

David cries out to God for help (v. 1). We don't know the circumstances, but he effectively asks God, 'Have I really deserved all this?' (vv. 2–5). After all, he has tried to speak the truth (v. 1), he hasn't plotted to do any evil (v. 3) or accepted bribes and he has not (at least in this instance) resorted to violence (v. 4). Generally, he has tried to follow God's ways (v. 5). Clearly David is not claiming to be sinless. His many failings recorded in Scripture and his prayers for forgiveness (see for example Ps. 51) make that clear. But he is grappling with a sense of injustice.

His appeal to God as his judge (vv. 2–5) changes into a prayer to the God who loves and protects him (vv. 6–9). He is confident that God answers prayer and will save him from his enemies (v. 6). He asks, 'Show me the wonders of your great love' (v. 7).

Opposition (vv. 10–14)

David then introduces the opposition: arrogant people with hard callous hearts (v. 10). They are out to get David, 'like a lion hungry for the prey' (v. 12). He urges God to rise up and save him, destroy his enemies and deal justly with them (vv. 13–14). He closes with the strong personal conviction, 'As for me …' (v. 15). Whether vindicated in this life or not, David was confident that he will see God face to face and find ultimate fulfilment in a relationship with him which goes on after death (see also Ps. 16:9).

REFLECTION

Read also 1 John 3:2 and 2 Corinthians 3:18. Notice the same confidence that we will see God face to face and be changed to become like him.

DAY 18

The Rock and the Rescuer

Think back in your life to a particularly difficult situation. How would you describe the experience of coming though that? Perhaps like going through a dark tunnel into the light or having a heavy load lifted from your back. As David looks back to his dark experiences, he uses powerful poetic images to describe his situation: 'The cords of death entangled me' ... 'The cords of the grave coiled around me' (vv. 4–5). He recalls God's rescue in answer to prayer: 'he drew me out of deep waters' (v. 16), and the result: 'He brought me out into a spacious place' (v. 19). It's a very attractive picture of freedom and enjoyment.

After sharing so many of his problems in the first 17 psalms (1, 8, 10 and 16 excepted), David looks back with thanksgiving for what God has done for him and for all that God showed himself to be: a rock, a refuge and a rescuer (vv. 2–3). David loves the Lord who saved his life and so he wants to sing (vv. 1–3).

Verse 20–24 may seem strange to us. It seems David is almost congratulating himself on his good character which caused God to rescue him! But later statements tell us this is not the case. David knows that the Lord brings low the haughty and saves the humble (v. 27) and that we have no hope unless we 'take refuge in him' (vv. 30–31), and rely on the Lord for strength (vv. 32–35) and for help in overcoming our enemies (vv. 37–45).

The psalm ends with joyful praise that 'The LORD lives!' (v. 46) and he has continued to show his unfailing love (vv. 47–50).

REFLECTION

Take time to thank God for his saving power in your life through the death and resurrection of Jesus. He is our rock and our rescuer (v. 2).

 **DAY 19**

God has spoken

How can we know God? We cannot see him or touch him, but the Bible insists that we can know him because he has communicated with us and revealed himself. He has acted and he has spoken. Psalm 19 brings together in one song the truths that God has spoken in his creation (v. 1) and his word (v. 7), and he calls us to listen.

'The heavens declare ... ' (vv. 1–6)

As in Psalm 8, David looks up to the skies and ponders the unimaginable greatness of the God who made the universe. The creation speaks to us about the Creator. It is 'the work of his hands' (v. 1). It speaks every day in a universal language (v. 2). There is no verbal communication, but its 'voice goes out into all the earth' (v. 4; see also Rom. 1:20).

The Word of God (vv. 7–11)

As God speaks through his creation, so he speaks through his written word (v. 7). David's generation only possessed the Torah, (the first five books of what we call the Old Testament), commonly known as 'the Law', though it contains much more than laws. He ponders the qualities, purpose and value of God's Word. It is perfect, trustworthy, right, radiant and firm because it expresses the character of God (vv. 7–9). It is given to reveal God to us. The effect on the reader is also intended to be positive. It refreshes the soul, makes us wise and brings joy to the heart and light to the eyes. (vv. 7–9). It is 'more precious than gold' (v. 10).

David knows as he reads the Word of God that it also convicts him of his sin (vv. 11–13). So in the closing words of this song, he prays that all that he thinks and speaks will be pleasing to God (v. 14).

God has spoken supremely in and through Jesus Christ, to whom all the Old Testament writers bear witness (Heb. 1:1–3). If your study of the Bible has become dry, ask God to give you a greater hunger to read his Word, to understand it and to put into practice what you hear.

 **DAY 20**

Into battle

This psalm reads like a preparation for battle. As the king is about to lead his armies out to fight, the people pray for him, and for themselves, as they gather with him. When we read a psalm like this about the Lord's anointed, we are right to think of Jesus, the Christ (that is, anointed king). We are right to think of the battle he fought and won against the powers of darkness on the cross (Col. 2:14–15) and to look to him for strength in the spiritual battles we are called to fight (Eph. 6:10–12). Our King has won the decisive battle. Our destiny depends on him. His victory is our victory.

The psalm opens with five specific prayer requests to God for the Lord's anointed king (vv. 1–5). David prays that the Lord would:

1. answer the king when 'in distress' (v. 1);

2. help him (v. 2);

3. remember and accept his offerings (v. 3);

4. give the king the desires of his heart and make his plans succeed (v. 4); and,

5. grant that all the people would be able to celebrate his victory (v. 5).

As so often in the psalms, David then changes from prayer to confident statements of faith in God. David continues, 'Now this I know … ' (v. 6). What does he know? He is confident that 'The LORD gives victory to his anointed' (v. 6). He knows that God calls his people to trust him and not rely on external material aids or their own resources. (v. 7). Indeed, those who rely only on their own abilities and clever plans 'are brought to their knees and fall, but we [that is the faithful believers] rise up and stand firm' (v. 8).

REFLECTION

Notice how this psalm reminds the king and the people of their total dependence on God. They pray before going out to battle, they look to him alone for help (v. 9) and they remind themselves that no matter how well trained and resourced they may be, they rely on the Lord for victory (v. 9). There are some good lessons to learn here as we go out to live for the Lord each day (see Zech. 4:6), keeping our eyes on him (Heb. 12:1–3).

Rejoicing in victory

It's great to celebrate a victory, whether our own success, a big win by our favourite sports team or, more seriously, a victory in war. My parents' generation danced in the streets when the Second World War ended in 1945. Hitler's Nazi regime had been defeated and they had much to be thankful for; it was a great victory to celebrate after six years of conflict and hardship.

David knew he had much to celebrate when he wrote this psalm. The people had prayed *before* going out to battle (Ps. 20). This psalm is their victory song *after* the battle. It celebrates the king's relationship with the Lord (vv. 1–7) and the king's defeat of his enemies (vv. 8–12). It ends with the people's desire to exalt the Lord and to sing praise to him (v. 13).

The king and the Lord (vv. 1–7)

David knew it was the Lord who had given him the victory (v. 1). He had answered the king's prayers (v. 2) and blessed him (v. 3). The Lord had given him long life and honoured him (v. 5). The Lord had granted him 'unending blessings' and made him glad with the joy of his presence (v. 6). The king's security, indeed the people's security, comes only through trust in the Lord, in 'the unfailing love of the Most High' (v. 7).

The king's victory (vv. 8–12)

David celebrates that the Lord had enabled him to defeat and destroy all his enemies. There is a strong hint here of a much wider and greater victory over God's enemies than just the battles fought by David some 3,000 years ago. It foreshadows the victory of God's Messiah, Jesus.

REFLECTION

Christians have much to thank God for and much to celebrate. We look back to the death and resurrection of Jesus, to his decisive victory over sin, evil and death (see for example 2 Thess. 1:7–10). We look forward to celebrating the completeness of that victory in heaven and we enjoy now every experience of his presence that is a foretaste of that final victory. No wonder that Christian worship has always include joyful singing!

29

DAY 22

Suffering and victory

One man suffers and many enjoy the victory that results. That's what this psalm/prayer is about. We might summarise it like this:[4]

*LORD, why have you left me? You don't answer my prayers (vv. 1–2). **Yet** I know you have helped your people in the past (vv. 3–5) **but** I am suffering terribly (v. 6). People are laughing at me because I still trust you (vv. 7–8). **But** though you have been my God since the day of my birth you are not helping me **now** (vv. 9–11). I feel threatened, alone and in awful pain (vv. 12–18). **But** I look to you. Help me and I will tell others how you delivered me (vv. 19–25). I know that one day people everywhere will praise you (vv. 26–31).*

The cross

David must have been going through a terribly painful test of his faith. Through the inspiration of God, he also gives us an insight into the sufferings of the Messiah Jesus, who was to come. He pictures prophetically the crucifixion of Jesus in astonishing detail: his pierced hands and feet (v. 16); his raging thirst (v. 15); the hatred of the mob (vv. 12, 16); the dislocation of his bones (v. 14); and even the soldiers gambling for his clothes (v. 18). He shows us the spiritual agony of our suffering Saviour, utterly alone, crying out from the cross the opening words of this psalm, 'My God, My God, why have you forsaken me?' (Matt. 27:46).

The big question: 'why?'

Why did God allow Jesus, his only Son and the most perfect human being who has ever lived, to die an agonising and shameful death? It was for us (Is. 53:1–6). Jesus died on our behalf, in our place, the just for the unjust to bring us back to God (vv. 25–31).

REFLECTION

This psalm also expresses the pain of believing people in every generation who suffer wthout cause and ask God 'why?' Let this psalm drive us to Christ, who suffered and died for us.

The Shepherd and the feast

Confidence in the future; contentment in the present. These are two very rare and elusive qualities in our world. As we are beset by worries about the future of our world, our families and our own lives, and as we join the rat race continually chasing after 'more', this most famous of all psalms speaks powerfully to us. It is often called the 'Shepherd psalm', but it actually paints two pictures for us: the Lord as the good shepherd (vv. 1–4) and the Lord as the host of a great feast (v. 5).

The Good Shepherd

Ancient Israel had many poor leaders who were supposed to lead and 'shepherd' the people, but who failed miserably (see Jer. 23:1; Ezek. 34:2, 6). By contrast, God himself is the Good Shepherd. He cares, provides, protects and leads (vv. 2–3). Secure in that knowledge, the psalmist contentedly concludes, 'I lack nothing' (v. 1).

The Good Shepherd also always leads us to do that which is consistent with his name and character (v. 3), even though we often wander off like foolish sheep (Is. 53:6). Even in the dark times, even in death, the Good Shepherd is still with us (v. 4). Notice how personal this psalm gets, as it changes from statements *about* God (vv. 1–3) to speaking directly *to* God (v. 4).

The victory feast

The picture changes from the protection of a rural shepherd to a great victory feast with the Lord himself as the host (v. 5; see also Luke 22:16). There is a common theme between these two very different pictures. The Lord himself takes total responsibility for caring and providing for us: as a shepherd for his sheep, and as a gracious host for his friends.

REFLECTION

The psalm ends on a great note of confidence: 'Surely your [God's] goodness and love will follow me all the days of my life, and I will dwell in the house of the LORD for ever' (v. 6). 'Surely' here is not a hopeful expression, nor just wishful thinking. It's a statement of certainty based on the promise of God, which lasts on into eternity.

 **DAY 24**

Access and acceptance

Psalm 24 was most likely a processional song, used originally by David as he brought the ark to Jerusalem (2 Sam. 6), and later by worshippers progressing into the city and on into the tabernacle or temple. It's the third in the trilogy of Psalms 22, 23, 24, each of which portrays a different view of the coming Messiah. He is the Saviour who suffers (Ps. 22), the Good Shepherd (Ps. 23) and the Sovereign (Ps. 24).

It opens with a majestic view of God, the Creator of all (vv. 1–2), and goes on to ask and answer two big questions: not 'why?' (Ps. 22) or 'how long?' (Ps. 13), but rather …

'Who may ascend the mountain of the LORD?' (vv. 3–6; see also Ps. 15)

David asks, 'Who may stand in his holy place?' (v. 3). In other words, he is asking all of us, 'Who is fit to stand in the presence of the Holy God, the great Creator?' The answer: 'The one who has clean hands and a pure heart' (v. 4) … 'They will receive blessing … and vindication' (v. 5). Can any of us claim to make the grade? No! It is only by the mercy and grace of God, and not by our own goodness or efforts, that any of us are accepted (see Ps. 12 and Rom. 3:23). David understood that, at least in later life (see Ps. 51).

'Who is the King of glory?' (vv. 7–10)

David calls out to the city to open its gates to welcome its returning 'King of Glory' (v. 7). But twice he asks, 'Who is the King of Glory?' (vv. 8, 10) and in each case receives the answer that it is not David or any earthly successor, but 'The LORD Almighty – he is the King of glory' (v. 10). It is the Covenant God of Israel, the Creator of the earth who is also the great King. By his grace he allows sinful people, with unclean hands and impure hearts, to enter and enjoy his holy presence and share in the spoils of his victory.

REFLECTION

What encouragement do we find in the New Testament about access to God and acceptance by God? See Romans 5:1–8 and Hebrews 4:14–16.

Running away to God

'When you feel like running away, run away to God.' This wise advice was given to me at a time when life seemed particularly difficult. When we want to 'run *away* from it all', we are wise to run *to* our heavenly Father, who understands us and who will set us back on our feet.

Problems

David must have felt like running away. He had treacherous enemies who hated him (vv. 2–3, 19). He felt lonely, sinful and very troubled (vv. 15–18). But he doesn't run away from his problems; he runs to God with them. He then stands and faces them, as he had faced Goliath, armed with the strength of God that he drew from prayer (vv. 1, 5, 15, 21).

Looking to the Lord

David's life, with all its pressures, was orientated towards God. He prays urgently for God to protect him, to teach him, to guide him and to 'remember' (as if he might forget!) his great mercy and love (vv. 2–6). In particular, as his mind keeps turning back to his own sinfulness, he asks God to forgive him (vv. 7, 11, 18) and to strengthen his character (v. 21). Finally, he prays for all the people of God who are in trouble (v. 22).

Sandwiched between his requests, he meditates on the character of God. He is good and righteous, even towards sinners like us. He guides and teaches the humble (vv. 8–10) and befriends and confides in those who fear him (v. 14). Verse 15 paints a great word picture of what it means to 'look to the LORD': like a child whose feet get stuck in the mud and who looks to their parent to lift them out, or like an animal whose feet are caught in a trap, so David looks to the Lord for help.

REFLECTION

David's thoughts in this prayer seem to ebb and flow between need and assurance. As we pray, perhaps, like David, our thoughts move from our problems – to God – to our circumstances – and finally back to God who is able and willing to meet our need.

DAY 26

In the presence of God

If you love someone, you want to be with them and enjoy spending time with them. So for David worship is not a religious duty. He delights to be in the house of God, in the presence of God, because he loves God (see also Ps. 27:4 and 28:2). His personal devotion shines through this psalm.

Self-righteous?

'Vindicate me, LORD, for I have led a blameless life' (v. 1). How are we to understand these opening words, repeated in part in verse 11? Is David claiming his own merit and goodness to earn his acceptance with God? Is he claiming to be without fault and without sin? How do we equate these words with his very different assessment of his life in Psalms 32 and 51?

The opening verses help us understand what David is saying. He trusts in the Lord (v. 1). He well knows his dependence on God's unfailing love and faithfulness (v. 3). He also shares the Lord's hatred of evil and deceit (vv. 4–5). He asks God to test him, to try him and to examine his heart (v. 2). He wants to be honest with God, rather than hide behind a cloak of hypocrisy (v. 4).

Devotion

What underlies the psalm is not moral pride or self-righteousness, but rather David's devotion to the Lord, which takes up much of the second half of this psalm (vv. 8–12). His appeal to God throughout is based on dependent loyalty, not on self-righteousness. So he prays for God to spare his soul (v. 9), to deliver him and to be merciful to him (v. 11).

He loves to be consciously in the presence of God: 'I love the house where you live, the place where your glory dwells' (v. 8; see also Ex. 40:35). He wants to praise God and tell others of what God has done (vv. 6–7). As he comes to the house of God, he stands on level ground with all the rest of God's people in his desire to praise and honour the Lord.

REFLECTION

What does it mean for the Christian to say, 'I love the house where you live' (see Eph. 2:19–22)?

Fear and confident faith

In this statement of faith, David reminds himself (and us) that because God is both a light and a strong deliverer, he has nothing to fear. He was going through a bad experience. He felt cut off from God. He was afraid, under attack from 'evil men' (vv. 2–3) and surrounded by enemies (v. 6). That's why this psalm, and others like it, speak to us powerfully when we feel that evil is all around and that the world is lined up against us. It reminds us of the reality and power of God and all he has promised to be and to do in our lives.

Light in the darkness (vv. 1–3)

Here David is effectively saying, 'The Lord is my light in the darkness and my salvation for this situation in which I am so fearful.' Sometimes the evil in this world can seem overwhelming, but the darkness can never defeat God and his good purposes for our life.

Fulfilment (vv. 4–6)

In the midst of his troubles, David sees his priorities very clearly: 'One thing I ask from the LORD' (v. 4). There is no experience so fulfilling and ultimately satisfying as to 'gaze on the beauty of the LORD' to experience the security of knowing God as our refuge and strength (v. 5). That generates a great joy from deep within us that makes us want to sing (v. 6).

Tested faith (vv. 7–10)

Even in David's single-minded devotion to God, his faith is still tested as he cries out to God in prayer (vv. 7–8), feeling lonely and forsaken, and needing God to guide him through a maze of difficulties and intense oppositon (vv. 9–10).

Confident faith (vv. 13–14)

This psalm ends with one of the most wonderfully encouraging statements of faith to be found in all Scripture: 'I remain confident of this: I will see the goodness of the LORD in the land of the living' (v. 14).

REFLECTION

Note this psalm moves from security and satisfaction back to struggle before ending in confidence. Sometimes our life experience is like that. Our moods and circumstances may change, but God's love and faithfulness is constant.

 **DAY 28**

Deliverance from fear

Fear can grip us: fear of pain; fear of loneliness; fear for our children; fear of the future; fear of death itself. Such fear can paralyse us and oppress us. David shares with us his biggest fear in this psalm. It is fear of being 'like those who go down to the pit' (v. 1). He prays to God, 'Do not drag me away with the wicked' (v. 3). He is fearful not only of death but of God's rejection – of being counted among those who have 'no regard for the deeds of the LORD' (v. 5).

So David cries out to God for mercy (v. 2), for judgement on the evil doers (v. 4) and for salvation, not just for himself but for all the people (v. 9). He turns to God as his Rock (v. 1), a familiar theme in the psalms. We are to picture a rocky outcrop, high on a hill, a vantage point and a place of safety from enemies looking to attack. The Lord is also David's strength and his shield (v. 7). The Lord is both an enabler and a protector.

As David lifts his eyes beyond his own fears, he prays for others. Indeed, as the Lord's anointed, his responsibility before God is to act for the good of the people. David affirms that 'The LORD is the strength of his people, a fortress of salvation for his anointed one' (v. 8). As the Lord protects his anointed leader, so the people will be protected.

The final picture is of God as a shepherd of his people (see also Ps. 23), who carries the sheep who are especially vulnerable to attack. Note that he carries them 'for ever' (v. 9; see also Is. 63:9).

REFLECTION

This psalm reminds us of the many facets of the grace of God experienced by all who look to him and trust in him. He is our Rock, our fortress, our shield, our strength and our shepherd. As we ponder these truths, so, like David, we will be delivered from our fears.

The glory and grace of God

We human beings may stand in awe at the powerful forces in creation – the oceans, volcanoes, waterfalls, high mountains – but this psalm lifts our eyes to the awesome power of the Creator God.

This is an extraordinary psalm. It's very different to the prayers to God for help or confessions of sin that characterise many of David's psalms. There is not a single 'prayer request' in all the psalm. Rather it is a glorious exaltation of Almighty God.

God's name, Yahweh (translated as 'Lord' in most English Bibles), is used 18 times in 11 short verses. It is a repeated reminder that this almighty deity is not unknown, but is the God who revealed himself to Moses and who bound himself by covenant to the people of Israel. It opens with a vision of heaven, then changes to a view of the majestic power of God and concludes with the Lord's blessing on his people.

Worship in heaven (vv. 1–2)

Here is David, a mere human being, so taken up in worship as to exhort the angels in heaven (v. 1) to honour God, giving him 'the glory due his name' (v. 2). His name means the revelation of his divine character.

We hear the 'voice of the Lord' (vv. 3–19)

The Lord's voice speaks over the waters (v. 3); the thunder (v. 3); the great cedars of Lebanon, emblems of strength and durability (v. 5); Sirion, the mountain of Hermon (v. 6); the desert (v. 8); the great oak forests (v. 9); and the flood (v. 10). God speaks into, and over, his great creation. He is 'enthroned over the flood' (v. 10) – most likely a reference to Noah's flood (Gen. 6–8). He is greater than any of the powers and forces he has built into his creation. Of course he is! He made it all!

The Lord and his people (v. 10)

The Lord gives strength to his covenant people and 'blesses his people with peace' (v. 11).

REFLECTION

It is this great God of all the earth, not some localised tribal God or some unknowable spirit power, who has revealed himself to us in Jesus Christ (John 1:18).

37

Turning sorrow into joy

Remembering how God has helped us in the past, especially answering our prayers in difficult times, and thanking him is a great way to deepen our relationship with him and so find strength to face the future. After the glory of Psalm 29, this psalm takes us back to the more familiar territory of David struggling and crying out for God's help, yet thankful for God's past goodness to him and finding in the Lord great joy and confidence for the future.

Thanksgiving (vv. 1–3)

David had prayed for deliverance (Ps. 28). He now thanks God for answering his prayer: 'you lifted me out of the depths and did not let my enemies gloat over me' (v. 1). David's life was in danger, but the Lord saved him.

Testimony (vv. 4–5)

David turns from prayer to testimony. He shares with the people, and with us, his experience of God's goodness. He encourages us to sing praise to God because he is gracious. Even the darkest human experiences have a joyful end for the faithful believer (v. 5; see also 2 Cor. 4:17).

Prayer (vv. 6–10)

David reflects on times past when God favoured him, when his life was strong and stable (v. 6), but then tells the Lord, 'when you hid your face, I was dismayed' (v. 7). So he cries to God for mercy and asks, 'What is gained if I am silenced, if I go down to the pit?' (v. 9). His logic leads him to think that it's better for God to rescue him so that he can testify to God's faithfulness. He is more use alive than dead! Whether or not that is so for David (or for any of us) is of course only for God to decide. In any event this reflection turns David back to pray for help (v. 10).

REFLECTION

'... weeping may stay for the night, but rejoicing comes in the morning' (v. 5). Perhaps you can relate to these words when you look back to dark times when God has helped you. The change God made in David's life (vv. 11–12) made him want to praise God from his heart – and to praise God forever (v. 12).

DAY 31

Highs and lows

A succession of highs and lows: sometimes our experience of life is like that. At times, we may be very conscious of God's blessing on our life, enjoying a sense of his presence and answers to our prayers, but our circumstances and mood can quickly change. Problems come, doubts arise and suddenly we feel God is far away. But God does not change. He is totally faithful.

David's experience

In this psalm, David's experience seems like a rollercoaster. After urgent prayer (vv. 1–2), leading to deliverance and thanksgiving (vv. 3–8), David is in a good place (v. 8). But then it looks like he goes back to square one (v. 9). David takes us through the whole process again (vv. 9–24), from pain and anguish (v. 10), back to renewed confidence in God (vv. 23–24). He is in severe distress (vv. 9–13). Every part of his body is affected (vv. 9–10). He is an object of contempt by his neighbours; nobody wants to know him (vv. 11–12). Indeed, they are plotting against him (v. 13). But he continues to trust in the God who rules his life (vv. 14–15). He longs to know again the smile of God on his life (v. 16) and to see the lying lips of the wicked being silenced (vv. 17–18).

God the Rock

By contrast to our changing moods and circumstances, God is a refuge and strong fortress: a place of safety when under attack (vv. 1–4). David asks God to be his rock and refuge (v. 2) and then affirms that God *is* his rock and fortress (v. 3). He is faithful and trustworthy (v. 5). He is lovingly, totally committed to us (vv. 7, 16). So we can totally entrust our lives to him (v. 5).[5]

The psalm ends on a strong note of thanksgiving and praise (vv. 19–21) with an encouragement to others to 'Love the Lord' (v. 23) and to 'Be strong and take heart' (v. 24).

REFLECTION

Note the turning point in David's experience (v. 14). Relying on God gives us rock-solid security and renewed strength whatever our situation or feelings.

Forgiven and restored

When we damage a relationship with someone we love, through our hurtful words or actions, it usually leaves us with a sense of guilt, of deep unrest and of pain. Our conscience troubles us. We don't feel good about ourselves, however much we try to justify our positon. But when we ask for forgiveness and receive it, then peace is restored to the relationship, as well as to our own hearts.

So it is in our relationship with God. Our sins separate us from him. We can have no rest or peace until we have acknowledged that sin, repented of it, and sought and received God's forgiveness. The experience of joy and deep sense of 'rightness' that comes from being reconciled to God is the main theme of this psalm.

David knew he had broken God's laws (v. 1). He also knew that this was not an occasional lapse from the norm of good behaviour. He had a deeper problem called 'sin', something rotten at the core of his being (vv. 1–2). He tells us, in very emotion-charged language, the experience of carrying a burden of guilt and unconfessed sin (vv. 3–4). He goes on to share the experience of forgiveness and relief that came from owning up to

his sin after first attempting to deny it (v. 5). He recounts his deep happiness of being forgiven by God – of having his sin taken away, covered and no longer counted against him (vv. 1–2).

No wonder David urges us to seek God for ourselves (v. 6). No wonder he celebrates not only that God has forgiven him, but also that God protects him and delivers him (vv. 7–8). But God also has something to say. He will lovingly teach David how he wants him to live, if only he will listen and learn (vv. 8–9).

REFLECTION

Read Isaiah 53:4–6, which helps us understand more deeply the amazing love of God (vv. 10–11) and how the Holy God can forgive our sins. Notice also how Paul quotes these verses in Romans 4:7–8 when writing about justification by faith in Jesus Christ.

God's world and God's people

Sometimes we forget the basics. This psalm (like Ps. 103) reminds us and celebrates the most basic wonderful truths of all: this is God's world and we (believers from every nation) are his people.

After so many psalms in which David shares his struggles of faith, this song of praise to God for who he is, and for what he has done, comes like a shaft of sunlight in the dark. The unnamed author calls us to join him in praising God with our voices, with musical instruments and with shouts of joy (vv. 1–3).

Reasons to praise God (vv. 4–7)

Why should we praise God? His word is true and 'he is faithful in all he does' (v. 4); he 'loves righteousness and justice' and 'the earth is full of his unfailing love' (v. 5); and he is the great Creator (vv. 6–7). This is God's world. He made it all by the power of his spoken word (Gen. 1).

Who should praise him? (vv. 8–15)

All the peoples of the world owe God worship (v. 8) because he is the Creator of all (v. 9). The 'nations' who do not acknowledge God (see Ps. 2:1) find that it is the Lord who is ultimately in control whatever plans they make (vv. 10–11). He sees *all* mankind (v. 13); he watches *all* who live on the earth (v. 14); he forms the hearts of *all* and considers *everything* they do (v. 15).

But it is the people who know him as Lord – who know his salvation and love, and who put their trust in him – who have particular reasons to praise him (vv. 12, 18–20). See also Ephesians 2:1–10 and 1 Peter 1:1–5.

REFLECTION

Who can we rely on (vv. 16–22)? This psalm reads like a lesson learned from hard experience rather that an academic theory or pious hope. Ultimately reliance on our own resources and abilities will not guarantee success (see also Ps. 20:7). Rather, patient trust in the Lord is the way forward for all God's people in every age (vv. 18–22): 'We wait in hope for the LORD; he is our help and shield' (v. 20).

DAY 34

Answered prayer

It's good to look back and recall answers to prayer. It's good to share those experiences with others: it honours God, it strengthens our faith and it may help others to 'taste and see' for themselves that the Lord is good (v. 8).

This psalm is David's testimony to God's answer to his prayer for help in a desperate situation. The heading tells us that David wrote it after he had escaped from the court of the Philistines. He was being threatened by his enemies and feigned madness to escape (1 Sam. 21:10–15). Looking back on this low point in his life, when his faith nearly failed him, he concluded that God had heard his cry for help and delivered him from this life-threatening situation. So he wrote this psalm about the goodness of the Lord who answers prayer (vv. 6, 17).

This psalm is not a prayer: there is not a single line addressed to God. Rather, it:

- begins with a commitment to praise and glorify the Lord (v. 1);
- tells what David has learned about the character of God (vv. 5, 15);
- tells of answers to prayer (vv. 4, 18, 19); and
- ends with the confidence that God will rescue all who serve him and take refuge in him (v. 22).

David encourages all who will listen to seek God and experience for themselves the goodness of God (vv. 8, 10). He calls us to join him in honouring God (v. 4), and to trust him and prove for ourselves that he will help us and save us despite all our failings (v. 8, 22).

God invites us to pray to him. Perhaps we only call on him from time to time – when it suits us, when we remember or when we are in real trouble – but, as David found, God is always listening.

REFLECTION

What is your 'testimony' about how God has helped you in the past and answered prayer?

God's timetable ... God's ways

When people hurt us, our natural human response is to want to hit back. If they hurt us without cause and with malicious intent, then we have double the reason to respond in kind. We might also ask God – in frustration and anger, and with a burning sense of injustice – *why* he has allowed it to happen and *how long* we have to wait before he rights the wrongs done to us. In such situations we may have to learn painful lessons. God does not 'jump to perform' to meet our timetable and expectation. He is God. Faith in him will always be tested, especially in difficult times, like precious gold refined in the fire (1 Pet. 1:7).

What does David ask God to do?

He wants God to contend for him against his enemies (vv. 1, 23) and to vindicate him (v. 24), because he has been unfairly treated. He also wants God to punish his enemies because they are plotting evil against him (vv. 3–8, 11–16, 19–22, 26–27). What action does God take? We are not told! What we do know is that he continues his work of grace in David's life through this experience.

Unanswered prayer?

To David, it seemed like his prayers had gone unanswered for a long time (v. 13). When life seemed to be inflicting some harsh blows and yet God was not coming to the rescue, like most of us he found it difficult just to wait. Like us, his view of how injustices should be sorted out was imperfect. But he knew that if *he* took revenge it was likely to make matters worse rather than better.

Like us, he had to learn that it is through faith *and patience* that we inherit the promises of God (Heb. 6:12) and that God's ways are not our ways (Is. 55:8), to which we might add that neither is his timetable the same as ours. Sometimes we have to wait, trust him and not take matters into our own hands (Ps. 27:14).

REFLECTION

On our desire to demand immediate justice when we are treated unfairly, read Romans 12:17–21.

Evil and the power of God

Sometimes the power of evil in our world seems overwhelming. As the 24-hour news cycle brings us war, cruelty, corruption and political stupidity, we can easily sink into despair and take our eyes off God. This psalm opens with David in this condition (vv. 1–4). He describes 'the wicked'. They do not fear God (v. 1); they flatter themselves to the extent that they are no longer aware of their own sin (v. 2); their words are 'wicked and deceitful' and 'they fail to act wisely or do good' (v. 3); even when they lie down to rest they are planning more evil and committing themselves to doing it (v. 4). It's not a pretty picture, but it's a realistic description of how sin affects our thoughts (v. 2), our words (v. 3) and our actions (v. 4), and how low we human beings can get when we throw off all constraints and try to dispense with God himself (see also Rom. 1).

Then what a change as David turns to focus fully on the Lord: 'Your love, LORD, reaches to the heavens' (v. 5). He celebrates the love, faithfulness, righteousness and justice of God, which is greater than anything we can measure or imagine (vv. 5–7). God will protect those who respond to his love like a mother bird protecting her young under her wings (v. 7). He will provide not just the bare necessities but enough to enjoy and celebrate (v. 8). Furthermore, God is the source and sustainer of all 'life' and 'light' (v. 9), symbolising goodness, truth, justice and love (see also John 1 and 1 John 1 for more on these themes).

David concludes with a prayer, first for others (v. 10) and then for himself that he would not be defeated by proud or evil people (v. 11), and finally a statement of victory: evil will not triumph in the end (v. 12).

REFLECTION

This psalm contrasts 'the wicked' (v. 1–4) with the Lord (vv. 5–12): there will be only one winner in this contest (v. 12). As Jesus reminded us in the Lord's Prayer, it is God's name, God's will and God's kingdom that will prevail.

'Don't Fret ...'

'Don't let it upset you ... Don't worry about it!' We commonly dispense this sort of advice to friends or family members who have been slighted or unjustly treated, or who are anxious about the seeming success of arrogant or corrupt people. They are words easily spoken, but much harder to act on. Once anxiety gets a grip, it can be hard to shake off.

This psalms begins: 'Do not fret because of those who are evil' (v. 1; see also v. 7), but these are not just empty words. David gives us good reasons why we should stop envying their apparent success. Why? Because they will soon be gone (vv. 2, 9–10, 36); their day of reckoning is coming (v. 13); their power will be broken (v. 15); and, ultimately, they will be completely destroyed (vv. 20, 28, 38).

Like Psalm 1, David contrasts this terrible, future state of 'the wicked' with the glorious future of 'the righteous'. They will inherit the land (vv. 9, 11, 22, 29; see also Matt. 5:5). They are under the Lord's care and have a lasting inheritance (v. 18). They will be provided for (vv. 19, 25) and will themselves be generous (v. 26).

They have the law of God in their hearts (v. 31). God will deliver them from evil (v. 33), will keep them from falling (v. 24) and will give them a glorious future (v. 37).

So David encourages us to turn our anxious thoughts to God: to trust him, take delight in him, commit our way to him (vv. 3–5) and take refuge in him (v. 40). He commands us, 'Turn from evil and do good' (v. 27). As we do that, we have God's promise that he will vindicate us (v. 6) and deliver us (vv. 39–40). Finally, David adds his own testimony to reinforce the truth that the wicked have no future, but God looks after his own (vv. 25–26, 35–36).

REFLECTION

This psalm commands us, 'do not fret – it leads only to evil' (v. 8). The more we keep fretting about evil, the more likely we are to add to the world's evil rather than reduce it! See also James 1:20 and Romans 12:21.

Laid low in the dust

This prayer of David is very different to those we have seen where David is pleading the rightness of his cause (see for example Ps. 18 and 26), or where he can't understand why he is experiencing so much opposition and stress when evil people are prospering (37:1).

Here David is very low indeed. He is conscious of guilt (v. 4), of physical sickness and pain (vv. 5–7) and of mental and spiritual depression (vv. 8–10). His friends and neighbours are avoiding him and even planning his further demise (vv. 11–12). Worst of all, he feels that God is angry with him (v. 3) and that God himself is punishing him: 'Your arrows have pierced me, and your hand has come down on me' (v. 2). David is so low that he feels unable to speak and even to hear (v. 13). Perhaps hardest of all to bear is the prospect of his enemies gloating over his downfall (v. 16) and falsely accusing him of wrong (vv. 19–20).

It's hard to read this psalm without relating this to Jesus, the Lord's anointed, who experienced not only extreme physical and mental suffering, but also the wrath of God on our behalf (Rom. 3:25). His friends forsook him; his enemies accused him falsely of wrongdoing, plotting against him and gloating over his (apparent) downfall as he suffered the agony of the cross.

Though the sufferings of Jesus were unique, because they atoned for our sin, we may well share in 'the fellowship of sharing in his sufferings' (Phil. 3:10).[7] Certainly we are all subject to the stresses and pains common to all human beings. As believers, we may also suffer injustice and persecution just for being a Christian. In such situations we can find strength in the words of this psalm.

REFLECTION

Notice how the psalm ends. Even though David is feeling totally alone and in deep trouble, he still cries out to God, 'LORD [Yahweh] … my God … my Lord [Sovereign] and my Saviour' (vv. 21–22). This is a God he knows and trusts and so David finds comfort in that unchanging covenant relationship. Let's look and learn.

Lost and alone

It's a great relief to be honest with God, to tell him what we are really thinking and feeling, because, after all, he knows anyway! It is pointless to put on a cloak of religious hypocrisy and pretend to ourselves, and others, that life is good when it isn't; that we are cruising through life victoriously when we aren't; and that we are experiencing God's answers to our prayers when it feels like we are not.

This psalm is a breath of honesty. How wonderful it is that God understands how desperate we can sometimes feel and gives us songs and poems like this that echo our deepest thoughts. This psalm is a precious gift to us when we are at our lowest.

David had been bottling up his thoughts and keeping his mouth shut (vv. 1–3), but now he expresses himself with deep emotion. He has no problem telling God exactly how he feels.

First, he is conscious of his own mortality (vv. 4–6). Life is short and uncertain. What then, he asks, is the point of rushing around accumulating wealth when we don't know how it will be used after we have gone (v. 6)?

Second, he is conscious of his sin and of God's discipline in his life (vv. 9–11). He asks God to save him (v. 8) and to hear his prayer (v. 12).

Worst of all, he is feeling lost and alone in the world, and a stranger on earth (v. 12), soon to die and not enjoying life in the meantime. At this very low point he even asks God to leave him alone, to give up on him, so that he can find some enjoyment before he dies (v. 13). Thankfully God understands what is going on in our lives when we make requests like this, as Jesus understood Peter when he said something similar (Luke 5:8). But he will never leave us or forsake us.

REFLECTION

In the midst of all this angst, David still looks to the Lord. He still calls on God to listen (v. 12). Like a compass that points the way home when we are lost, David's hope still points steadfastly to the Lord.

DAY 40

'Out of the slimy pit' ... deliverance, obedience and dependence

In Psalms 38 and 39, we saw David learning to trust God in the face of severe problems, patiently waiting for God's deliverance. In this psalm David looks back with thanksgiving. He had waited patiently and God has delivered him! So he encourages us to wait on the Lord, to keep trusting him when times are tough.

Deliverance (vv. 1–5)

David testifies that God had answered his prayer when he was down in the pit, stuck in the mud and mire (v. 2) of sin, depression, opposition and desperate need. God had lifted him out, put him back on a solid footing (v. 2) and put a new song in his heart and in his mouth (v. 3). Looking back, David realised that his experience could also be an inspiration to others: 'Many will see and fear the Lord and put their trust in him' (v. 3). He knows that he has been blessed, as are all who look to the Lord for help (vv. 4–5).

Obedience (vv. 6–10)

David follows with an extraordinary statement of total commitment and obedience. He realises that God values David's offering of himself, expressing an inward desire to obey God, more than any outward act of worship

he might offer to God at the temple (vv. 6–8). He is also surely foreshadowing the coming Messiah. In Hebrews 10:5–7 these verses are quoted at length to explain that Jesus' sacrifice of himself for our sins was once, for all and forever. He was obedient to his Father even to the point of death, he proclaimed God's salvation and he revealed God's love and faithfulness (vv. 9–10).

Dependence (vv. 11–17)

David is back in trouble, again needing help, again praying for God's mercy, love and protection (v. 11). This is both because of his own sinfulness, of which he is acutely aware (v. 12), and because his enemies are again out to kill him (vv. 14–15). Once again he is waiting on God: 'you are my God, do not delay' (v. 17). Once again he knows he is totally dependent on God.

REFLECTION

Think of the tough times in your life. In what ways has God delivered you through those situations? What have you learned about obedience and dependence?

Restoration

In times of sickness, pressure and difficulty we usually learn a lot about ourselves. We may also learn a lot about God. In this psalm David shares what he learned when he was sick (v. 8), surrounded by malicious people plotting his downnfall (vv. 7–8) and betrayed by his close friend (v. 9).

First, in verses 1–3, he shares his conviction that those 'who have regard for the weak' are blessed (v. 1). The Lord will deliver them (v. 1), protect them (v. 2) and restore them (v. 3).

Second, in verses 4–9, David looks back on his own sickness, and remembers how he had prayed to God for mercy and healing. His conscience had been troubling him; he had felt that his sickness was a direct result of his sin (v. 4). Job's friends made the same mistake, as did Jesus' followers (John 9:1–3).

David's enemies had been closing in on him (vv. 5–8), hoping he would die (v. 5), and spreading lies about him (v. 6) and rumours that David would not recover this time (v. 8). Even his close friend had turned against him (v. 9). Does this suffering of David, the anointed king, sound familiar? It should do. It points us to Jesus, who suffered far worse than David the malicious hatred of his enemies and even betrayal by one of his close freinds (John 13:18).

Third, in verses 10–13, David turns again to the Lord for help and restoration. He knows that God has answered prayer and healed him. Now he just wants to be in God's presence in this life and the next – forever (vv. 12–13).

This psalm closes the first of the five 'books' that make up the collection of 150 psalms we have in the Bible (see the introduction). Like all the five books, it ends with exhaltant praise to God (v. 13).

REFLECTION

One of the marks of true faith is that we continue to trust and worship God when all the cards seem to be stacked against us. This psalm, like many others, reminds us that there is blessing in the relationship in itself, not just because of what God may give us. Perhaps that's why it ends in praise.

Longing for God (1)

These two psalms belong together. They were written by a member of a group of temple musicians called the Sons of Korah. Both psalms express the thoughts and feelings of someone who is feeling very stressed and very low, but who longs to be closer to God.

Feeling down

The writer is talking to himself. Three times, like a chorus repeated in a song, he asks himself the same question: 'Why, my soul, are you downcast?' (42:5, 11; 43:5). Twice he asks, 'Why must I go about mourning?' (42:9 and 43:2). He is feeling down, but he can't quite put his finger on the reason why. To add to his sense of unease, his enemies are mocking him, asking why his God, if he is there, doesn't come to help him (42:3, 10).

Feelng downcast, disturbed and depressed (42:5), surrounded by deceitful and wicked people (43:1) and forgotten by God (42:9), he turns to God in prayer. He remembers that God's love is directed towards him by day and night (42:8). He continues to affirm his trust in God and encourages himself to keep trusting and hoping, knowing that God will satisfy his deepest longing: 'I will yet praise him, my Saviour and my God' (42:11).

REFLECTION

'Why ... are you downcast?' When we are down, we tend to listen to ourselves – to our moans and grumbling and criticisms – and wrap ourselves around with self-pity and discouraging thoughts. The way out is to talk to ourselves instead. In the psalms, talking to ourselves – reminding ouselves of God's Word, God's presence and God's unfailing love, and expressing our longing for God – is a sign of spiritual health and a way of lifting ourselves out of the pit of self-pity and depression.

Longing for God (2)

Today we turn again to these two wonderful psalms, which express a deep longing for God in terms of thirst and in a desire to be 'back home' in his presence.

Thirst

The psalmist 'thirsts' for God, like a deer longs for 'streams of water' from which to drink (42:1–2). The writer must have seen the effects of drought in nature, and he could identify that experience with the state of his own spiritual life. He feels dried up spiritually and is thirsty for an experience of God that would satisfy his deep longing (see also Ps. 143:6). Having known God, he knows that nothing else and no one else can quench his thirst for spiritual reality.

Home sickness

However adventurous we are, however much we enjoy travelling, we may get homesick and long to get back to familiar people and places. The Welsh have a very evocative word in their language to describe this deep longing for home: they call it *hiraeth*. This writer must have been experiencing something similar, but with a deeper, spiritual dimension.

This psalmist looks back, remembering better times when he was back home celebrating and worshipping with God's people (42:4). He also remembers that God's love is un-changing and unfailing (42:8), and encourages himself to keep trusting and hoping in God (42:5, 11; 43:5). He wants to get back to the house of God (43:4). His 'homesickness' is actually a deep longing for God.

Looking forward, he pleads with God to rescue him and vindicate him (43:1–2). But also at a much deeper level than that, he longs for God's light and faithful care to lead him 'home', back to God's mountain, God's temple, God's altar (43:3–4). He wants to be back in the presence of God. He wants to go home.

Unanswered questions

When we read of revivals, with many people turning to Christ, in past times or in other places, we might naturally ask, 'Lord, why are we not seeing you at work in such a mighty way in *this* generation and in *this* place? We have tried to be faithful to you and your Word. Lord, we long to see you work. Please do it again!'

This is the theme of Psalm 44. In Psalms 42 and 43 we saw *one person* looking back longingly to past joyful times. Here *the nation* is collectively looking back: it begins with 'we' not 'I'. It contrasts the past glories with the present dark situation. It asks 'why?' and it calls on God to 'wake up' and get to work (v. 23).

The past (vv. 1–3)

The psalmist looks back to the Exodus, the time when God delivered the Israelites from slavery in Egypt and led the next generation into the Promised Land. *Then* they seemed to win their battles; *then* they experienced God's presence; *then* God was fighting for them (v. 3).

The present (vv. 9–16)

But *now* ... it looked like God has deserted them. They have been defeated, plundered and scattered (vv. 9–12). They have become an object of scorn and derision (vv. 13–16). In effect the psalmist boldly prays in verses 9–12, 'Lord, *you* have done this ...;' 'you have rejected and humbled us ...' (v. 9).

Why? (vv. 4–8 and 17–22)

So why has God allowed these defeats? Why does God hide his face and forget their misery? (v. 24). It's not as if they had turned to other gods, in this instance at least (v. 20). Rather they have kept faith with God (vv. 4–8). So why are they suffering in this way?

Verse 22 seems to provide a clue, if not an answer: the suffering was 'for your sake'. Significantly, Paul quotes this verse when referring to the suffering endured by the apostles (Rom. 8:36). Such suffering wasn't a sign of God's anger; it was just part of the cost of following Christ in a fallen world, a battle scar from the fight.

REFLECTION

What are the battle scars being carried by God's people today? What battle scars are you carrying?

DAY 45

The king's wedding

The king is getting married. The temple musicians, the sons of Korah, write a special wedding song. As we might expect on such an occasion, the words of the song are very complimentary about the king, his character, his speech and his relationship to God (v. 2). There are also prayers for the king, that he would defeat his enemies (v. 5) and show the qualities of truth, humility and justice (v. 4), which reflect the character of God – as the anointed king of God's people was called to do. Attention then turns to the bride (vv. 10–12) with the reminder that her first priority will now be her husband rather than her family, just as the husband's primary allegiance is now to his wife (see Gen. 2:24).

At one level we could read this psalm as just an interesting historical poem, celebrating a royal wedding in a society long since gone. But we are stopped in our tracks by verses 6–7, where the king is addressed as 'God' whose throne 'will last for ever and ever'. It's one of the many instances in the psalms where Jesus, the King of kings and great King David's greater son, is prefigured. The New Testament letter to the Hebrews quotes verses 6–7 in its opening chapter in explaining how all the Scriptures point to the unique, divine status of the man Jesus (Heb. 1:8–9).

This psalm also invites us to remember that marriage in the Bible is a living picture of the relationship between God and his people (Jer. 2:2) and between Christ, the Bridegroom, and his church (Eph. 5:31–32). Perhaps Jesus was thinking of this psalm when he told the parable about 'a king who prepared a wedding banquet for his son' (Matt. 22:2).

REFLECTION

The psalm concludes by focusing on the future. The king's descendants would continue to reign as God had promised David (2 Sam. 7:11–16), but they were flawed leaders who failed to perform their role. It is King Jesus that the nations will praise forever and forever (v. 17) and whose 'wedding' with his people we will one day celebrate (Rev. 21).

Confidence in the midst of chaos

This psalm begins and ends with statements of confidence in Almighty God. He is our refuge (v. 1) and fortress (v. 11) – a place of safety to run to when under attack. He is our strength – the one who empowers us to turn and face opposition without fear (v. 2). He is also always 'with us' (v. 11; see also v. 1). The psalm makes this confident statement of faith in the face of massive problems and threats.

First, there is the prospect of chaos in the created order (vv. 2–3)

'... the earth give way and the mountains fall' (v. 2). There are earthquakes, volcanic eruptions and tsunamis, when everything we had thought to be firm and stable is moving under our feet.

Second, there is the picture of chaos in human society (v. 6)

'Nations are in uproar, kingdoms fall' (v. 6). All the established countries, societies and governments, which seemed so stable, are falling apart. There is revolution and disruption everywhere. In the midst of this chaos stands 'the city of God' (v. 4), a major theme in the psalms (see for example Ps. 48) and throughout the Bible. God is present among his people and supplies them with what they need (v. 4). Like the created order, his city will not fall (v. 5; literally, 'will not be moved': the same word in the original Hebrew as in v. 2) even in the face of attack by 'the nations'. Why? Because God, who brought the world into being by the Word of his mouth, now speaks into this chaos (v. 6).

The final verses of the psalm (vv. 6–11) paint a picture of the world yet to come, when God causes wars to cease (v. 9; see also Is. 11). Again God speaks: 'Be still, and know that I am God' (v. 10). At the end, it will be God who is exalted in all the earth, not those who fight against him (vv. 9–10).

REFLECTION

In all the chaos, and whatever the future holds, we can enjoy the same confidence as the psalmist that our security is to be found in our covenant-keeping God: 'The LORD ... the God of Jacob', who is always with us (v. 11).

God is King

Here is another psalm from the Sons of Korah, another song of exuberant praise to God. The king in this psalm is not David or one of his successors, but God himself: 'the great King over all the earth' (v. 2; see also vv. 6–7).[8]

The psalm celebrates the authority of God over all the world. He is the God of all the nations. This point is made repeatedly:

- He is the great King over all the earth (vv. 2, 7); and

- 'God reigns over the nations' (v. 8).

It also celebrates the great privilege given to the people of Israel – here called the 'pride of Jacob' (v. 4) – to know him and to be loved by him. Why did God choose to reveal himself to Israel? The Bible's answer is simply that he did because he loved them! (Deut. 7:7–8). We might equally ask why God should send his Son to save sinners. The Bible's answer? He did because he loved us, not because there is anything loveable in us (John 3:16).

This psalm celebrates much more than a relationship confined to a select few. It has a wider view which sees nations, those outside the people of Israel, coming to know and honour the God of Israel with the result that God is highly exalted (v. 9).The New Testament sees this plan unfolding with the spread of the Christian gospel around the world in fulfilment of God's promise to Abraham (Gen. 12:2–3) and in response to Jesus' command to go and make disciples of all nations (Matt. 28:19–20).

REFLECTION

The kingship of God was proclaimed by Jesus as being a present reality in his own person (Mark 1:15). The Bible promises that one day we will see God's kingdom in all its fullness. We pray, as Jesus taught us, 'your kingdom come'. One day it will. Jesus will be revealed as 'Lord of lords and Kings of kings' (Rev. 17:14). Then, as Isaiah prophesied, 'the earth will be filled with the knowledge of the LORD as the waters cover the sea' (Is. 11:9).

The city of our God

Most of the world's population live in cities. Some are beautiful and loved for their culture, history and architecture, or for their shops and entertainment. Others are less attractive, with high crime rates, traffic pollution and sprawling housing estates, unlovely and unloved.

Here the psalmist sings about his love for Zion, the city of Jerusalem, but he has a much bigger picture in sight than just a localised capital city. He celebrates 'the city of our God' (v. 1), 'the city of the Great King' (v. 2), 'the city of the LORD Almighty' (v. 8). The centrepiece of the city is the temple, a place of worship, where the people meditate on the unfailing love of God (v. 9) who is present among his people. (v. 3). The city is not great in itself; it is the Lord who makes it great by his presence. The city may *look* secure (vv. 12–13), but it is only the Lord who makes it so (v. 14).

The earthly city of Jerusalem was destroyed by the Babylonians in 587 BC. Why did God allow this? The Old Testament prophets had warned that judgement was coming because the people had broken their covenant with God, worshipped other gods and mistakenly relied on the mere presence of the temple as a sign of God's blessing (Jer. 7:4). Ezekiel was given a vision of the glory of the Lord departing the temple and the city because God's own people had rejected him (Ezek. 10:18).

Both the city and the temple were rebuilt, but were destroyed again in AD 70. Jesus wept over the city (John 11:35) because he foresaw its destruction as the inevitable result of the people's rejection of him (Matt. 23:37 – 24:2). But that isn't the end of the story. John was given a vision of 'the Holy City, the new Jerusalem' (Rev. 21:2–40), in which God will be present forever. We look forward to that day.

REFLECTION

The psalm ends rejoicing, not in the city but in God himself. The knowledge of him is to be passed on to each successive generation (v. 13), because 'this God is our God for ever and ever' (v. 14).

DAY 49

The wise and the foolish

Question: what will we leave behind when we die? Answer: everything! Why then do we try to find meaning in life in accumulating wealth that we cannot take with us? This is the question addressed in this psalm. It's a message for all of us (v. 1).

Like the book of Proverbs, this psalm begins, in verses 1–4, with a call to listen to some 'words of wisdom' (v. 3). These will be about life and death, and particularly the foolishness of accumulating wealth as a primary objective in life.

The rest of the psalm is in two parts, verses 5–12 and verses 13–20, with each section ending with the 'punchline' (vv. 12 and 20).

First, the psalmist asks why people would trust in wealth, which is so uncertain, and boast of their riches, which they will eventually lose (vv. 5–11). He makes the obvious point that however much wealth you have, you cannot 'buy off' death; you cannot pay God to have another 50 years of life (vv. 8–9). Both wise and foolish, and even the rich and famous, die in the end (vv. 10–11).

The second part of the psalm begins by pressing home this truth: the fate of all who trust in themselves and their riches is that they will die and decay, 'far from their princely mansions' (v. 14). Yet then he injects a wonderful note of hope with that powerful word 'but' – this is the hinge on which the psalm turns. 'But God will redeem me from the realm of the dead; he will surely take me to himself' (v. 15).

So with that message of hope for the faithful believer, he concludes, 'Do not be overawed when others grow rich' (v. 16). Remember, 'they will take nothing with them when they die' (v. 17). Also though they might attract the praise and envy of others because of their material success, they will never 'see the light of life' (v. 19).

REFLECTION

The psalm concludes by repeating the punchline: 'People who have wealth but lack understanding are like the beasts that perish' (v. 20). The psalmist is very keen that we get the message!

DAY 50

A surprise summons to judgement

This psalm, composed by Asaph[9], begins with a summons to God's court: 'The Mighty One, God, the LORD, speaks and summons the earth from the rising of the sun to where it sets' (v. 1). God is revealing himself in his glory (v. 2). He is coming, and he has something to say (v. 3). But then comes a surprise: the scene pictured in this psalm is not of God judging the unbelieving nations but of God judging *his own people* (vv. 4–6), those who have had the great privilege of receiving the law, of seeing God at work in their midst and to whom he has sent prophets to speak his word. As Jesus said, 'From everyone who has been given much, much will be demanded' (Luke 12:48). With privilege comes accountability (see 1 Pet. 4:17).

A call for truth in worship (vv. 7–15)

This is addressed to well-intentioned religious people, not those openly rebelling against God. The judge is not passing sentence. Rather he points to the shallowness and formality of their worship, and calls for truth and change.

A warning about hypocrisy (vv. 16–21)

This is addressed to 'the wicked person' (v. 16). These are also seemingly religious people, but God exposes their hypocrisy, as Jesus exposed the hypocrisy of the religious leaders of his day (Matt. 23). These people are happy to go through religious ceremonies and recite laws, creeds and prayers, and even make promises to God (v. 16), but God sees the reality: 'You hate my instruction and cast my words behind you' (v. 17). They hear God's words, but they do not listen. They happily break the commandments (vv. 18–20). Because God does not immediately act in judgement, they become complacent, confident that God is not overly concerned about their life or behaviour (v. 21). But now God calls them to account.

REFERENCES

1 This psalm seems to have been originally the second half of Psalm 9 but appears in our Bibles as a stand-alone psalm.

2 Paul quotes this verse when he argues that 'no one will be declared righteous in God's sight by the works of the law' (Rom. 3:20).

3 The header to this psalm tells us that it was written by David 'when the LORD delivered him from the hand of all his enemies and from the hand of Saul'. The whole of this psalm appears in its context in 2 Samuel 22.

4 I have highlighted the 'but's and 'yet's which appear at turning points in the psalm and which help us follow its flow.

5 These were also the final words of Jesus on the cross (Luke 23:46).

6 This is an an alphabetical acrostic poem – each of the 22 verses begins with one of the 22 letters of the Hebrew alphabet. It would have been a great aid for those wanting to memorise the psalm in the original language.

7 This wording is taken from the 1984 version of the NIV.

8 See also Psalms 93–100 on the theme of the kingship of God.

9 Asaph was a Levitical singer (1 Chr. 15:16–17).

MORE IN THIS SERIES

ROMANS
Momentous News
By David Cook
ISBN: 978-1-906173-24-1

MARK
The Suffering Servant
By Jeremy McQuoid
ISBN: 978-1-906173-55-5

DANIEL
Far From Home
By Justin Mote
ISBN: 978-1-906173-68-5

1 THESSALONIANS
Living for Jesus
By Julia Marsden
ISBN: 978-1-906173-67-8

PHILIPPIANS
Press Towards the Goal
By Kay Mumford
ISBN: 978-1-909611-31-3

GALATIANS
The Life I Now Live
By Peter Mead
ISBN: 978-1-910587-09-6

ACTS
To the Ends of the Earth
By David Cook
ISBN: 978-1-909611-02-3

EZEKIEL
For His Glory
By Peter Lau
ISBN: 978-1-909611-83-2

JOHN
Never Thirst Again
By David Cook
ISBN: 978-1-909611-30-6

and more at...  **10 Publishing**
a division of **10** ofthose.com

To place an order call: **0330 2233 423** email: **sales@10ofthose.com**
or order online: **www.10ofthose.com**

10Publishing is the publishing house of 10ofThose. It is committed to producing quality Christian resources that are biblical and accessible.

www.10ofthose.com is our online retail arm selling thousands of quality books at discounted prices.

For information contact: sales@10ofthose.com or check out our website: www.10ofthose.com